Convers...

A Guid...

Confused Planet

By

Danijela Kracun & Charles McFadden

© 2010 NelaBooks

Table of Contents

Conversations with a Light Being

A Guide to Being Peaceful on a Confused Planet

Background

Red and Krill are light beings from the 15th dimension. Red is our main contact. He is the light being that we speak to the most. We had been speaking to Red for about a year before writing this book.

We met and befriended an older lady who wants to remain anonymous who we will call "Betty" at a meditation group we frequented. After finding out that we wrote books and that we were very open minded to spiritual experiences Betty told us about her friend Red. Red is an actual being from another planet. He comes to our planet through a portal. We did not know what to think at first but Betty won us over when several predictions both personal and global that Red spoke of came true. After the predictions came true we began to meet with Betty and Red and we would have conversations. Betty could actually see and communicate with Red and she would be his go between and converse back and forth between us and Red.

It is an odd experience to be in his presence. Many times we would feel very spacey and expanded and time would fly by.

Many times we would not know what was talked about until we listened back to our recordings. Sometimes we would even have physical symptoms from our encounters with Red such as slight headaches and disorientation. We would often need to eat or sleep after the encounter. Betty can see and speak to other beings that come through the portal however Red is the main being she communicates with.

An interesting thing about Red is he seems to be an average guy from another planet. He does not come off as a savior or someone who knows it all. In fact, since we have been speaking to him he has told us many times he does not know the answers to some of the questions we have asked him. He did not even know the meaning of some of our words.

Red has a sense of humor which makes him likable. He has the feel of a friend. Once we asked him if the Ra group is a real extraterrestrial group. He did hear of Ra and he said yes they were. We asked him about other extraterrestrials that we had heard about that he did not know of and he joked and said to us "that is like me asking you if you knew who Bob from America is".

Red usually speaks very fast and sometimes speaks in a strange way. He says a lot of run on sentences, yet there is a funky poetic quality to the way he comes across. When we transcribe Red's words from our recordings, we try to keep it true to the way he speaks and as authentic as possible. So please allow some openness for his unique way of speaking our language.

We asked Red many of our own questions and questions from other people and he always gave good advice. After doing this for a while we decided to ask him what information he would like to tell humanity. This book is Red's answer and his message to humanity.

Red's Introduction

Red: I do not want to write a book about predictions. I feel that people should try to unify with nature and earth and not to try to be so separate from the earth. There is a shift of consciousness happening on your planet now. Humanity must raise their current consciousness and vibration to move forward. The shift is not something you need to avoid. By predicting something it will only cause people fear. Predictions cause anticipation and fear of what is going to happen. There comes a time when people try to avoid and prevent predictions and that is not what the shift is about. The shift is about incorporating the shift with your life and trying to move forward. There is a unity that will continue from one dimension to another, although the planet will still vibrate at the same three dimensional level, it will be different because within the 3D spectrum there are higher dimensions or levels of the 3D. So as you are incorporating the shift with your life many people will also be able to vibrate at that higher 3D level.

Humanity is going to need to have some skills to not be so afraid. This is something you need to hear and understand and you cannot tell someone what to do, but you act the way you want them to act and show them how to be rather than telling them you have to be this way. People are not going to accept being told how to be. It seems that on your planet advice taking is very difficult. So what you want to do is show them. Be a peaceful role model.

So the book I would imagine would be more like me showing you and telling you how to embrace the shift and this change and not to be so afraid of what the shift is going to represent.

I would like to write this book not only for humanity but all the beings on earth, all of the plants, animals and insects. The inclusion of all beings I find very important for the exchange that is going to happen with the shift.

I would really like for the people to know that once the shift does occur it is important especially at that time to preserve their animal and insect brothers. Do not be so afraid about finding food, where it is going to come from and start hording and trying to take advantage of the animal's vulnerability at that time. Protect them and know that this is something that humanity should preserve because the plants, animals and insects are also following their path to a higher vibration and changing into something that is better on their own level of consciousness just like humanity.

I am not trying to predict anything and I am not trying to tell humanity how they need to act and how they need to be. My advice is something that might help them with changing times.

Humanity has been experiencing a great number of changes throughout history. However, it seems that in the recent years the changes have been accelerating. Throughout these changes the most important thing to do is to just relax and to not have any fear because everyone is going to be exactly where they need to be at that time. You are exactly where you should be. Exactly where you need to be and there is no need to panic or fear.

There is no need to have to go out and try to do something. This is something that is not about doing. A lot of beings on your planet are attached to doing because you are so used to being busy and doing many things. You are used to not being nice and loving toward one another and that is going to be something that you will have to change. Many of these changes that you are going to be making are within you and not an outer change but it will affect all of the outer changes around you. So by focusing on yourself and by focusing on all of the inside of you that you can change that is how you will change the outside. You do need to change within and that change will have an effect on the whole planet. You do however have an effect on one another and you are a part of the one, a part of a very grand universe. Your actions on a global scale do affect not only the beings on your planet but also affect a lot of the beings in the entire universe. So what you want to do at this time when things are really changing and the planet is really changing herself, is to relax and go with the flow. The planet is trying to get to a higher vibration and so will you. You just need to remember that there is not much to do other then be the true self that you already are.

Remember to be loving and kind and compassionate. This is something that your beings have forgotten. You have forgotten that compassion, love, and kindness expands a lot further than just within your family. It must expand to people you do not know, to strangers. It has to be with all of the beings that live on your planet. It has to be with the plants, insects and animals. This is something that you really need to work on. Many of you are not kind to plants, insects and animals and you are not kind to one another. You are never going to get to a higher vibration if you are not kind to one another.

So, I guess what I am trying to say is that you do not have to do any of these things because the planet will do it for you, but it might be easier if you help. It might be easier for those human beings who are a lot more sensitive and moving higher to be able to move higher on this vibration. The planet will eventually shake off those who are not ready to move on to a higher vibration. You can make it a little bit easier on the whole by being more kind, loving and compassionate. That would be the right and the polite thing to do. What you want to do is focus on yourself and focus on how you can change yourself to be loving and kind and compassionate. That will affect everyone else and it will affect how your planet will move higher. The planet may not want to shake you off.

This shift is not a big deal. It is something that happens with every single planet in the universe. This shift is not something that just happens to your planet. On a very grand scale it happens to everybody. Everybody has different dimensions and vibrations and they have to rise within those particular dimensions and vibrations. Sometimes the rise itself is not an easy thing to do but overall it is something that is necessary. Everyone does not just get older in age but also more mature and that maturity is something that most beings in the universe strive to achieve. It is not something we think about. We just do it because it is time for us to grow in vibration. A caterpillar does not think about the process it is going through. It just does.

So I do not want this book to be about, this is what you have to do or predictions of what is going to happen. The planet will do what the planet needs to do regardless of where you are in your growth. The planet is not really going to care. I think it might be something that is easier for the people and the beings on your planet to know that there are certain things that you might want to work on that might be helpful for everyone making it an easier transition. Moving from one type of vibration to another, your planet will never be anything more than a 3D planet but within the 3D there are definitely steps and you might be vibrating at a higher 3D. This shift in vibration is something that is very important for the entire planet to do, not just the individual people. So the insects will go through it, the animals will go through it, everyone will go though it.

The shift might be easier if you are more loving and compassionate and relax more in nature and not focus on weapons and work and money, but focus on yourself. Not telling people what to do but paying attention to how you are toward other beings. So hopefully this book will be somewhat of a mini guide. Not necessarily predictions, not an "I AM TELLING YOU WHAT TO DO", but helpful hints.

I would like to touch upon the question of disease and how your cells are very familiar to a memory of a certain thing that might have happened in your life. Letting go of that memory will dissolve disease.

I will talk about the importance of sharing your energy with the planet and how the planet shares her energy with you. It is very important to exchange with the trees and grass. Everything that you have that looks like an inanimate object comes from nature. It is made from nature and you do exchange with it.

I would also like to talk about how it is important to allow the sun to be near you and to allow the sun to penetrate the body and the planet and not be afraid of the sun. It is not something scary. This communion with the sun is very important because you do get most of your nourishment from it.

I want to talk about food and how it is not all that necessary and the process of how you will progress regardless of food intake. Food is not something that you are going to feel like you are going to need very much longer and that is something you will start to feel more and more.

I also think that it is important to do a chapter on how you show people how they should be acting rather then telling them. Preaching never works. I hope this book does not come off as a preaching type of a book. Maybe this book will be something that may be very helpful to people. Maybe it will inspire people to change their life and work towards being a better person which will help the whole.

Also, I will talk about thinking patterns, because thinking is something that gets in the way of many humans and you have a lot of negative thinking that goes out into the whole collective consciousness. That negativity affects people's energies. It is something you might want to focus on. Pay attention to your thinking because you do not want a lot of negative thinking to affect you personally and many other people on different levels.

These are some topics I would like to cover and keep it light. Nothing too big, a small read. Remember I come from a place where we do not use books but I am doing this because I think it might be fun to do and I like spending time with you. So hopefully it will not be something that will be needed per say, but maybe the words will go into the consciousness of the majority and permeate and spread through the invisible energy force. This book may affect your planet. You never know.

Cellular Memory Attachment

Red: I want to talk about cellular memory and I want to talk about the attachment to cellular memory and how many humans on your planet have this attachment to cellular memory. They are either connected to something that must have happened in their past or future and they hardly ever connect to their period of now, the present moment. So when you hear a song or when you are remembering something about an ailment like your head hurts you attach it to a particular disease or a particular memory and that is something that clouds your cells. What your cells need to feel is a lot of freedom and they need to feel that expansion and they need to turn into light. That is what is going to help you raise your vibration. The clearing of cellular memory is what is going to help you heal your self and help heal the planet and move into a higher vibration level. So attachment to a particular memory is what causes the cells to be blocked and you have to learn how to unblock theses cells. Of coarse all of this will happen through time. The best thing to do is to allow it to happen. Do not force anything and rest in nature. Do not be fearful of anything. So when you get diagnosed with a disease, you are living on a 3D planet and you may not be ready to acknowledge what this disease is. It is an attachment to a memory that might have happened in a past life or it might have been something that you feared and brought the disease on somehow. If you can figure it out and somehow drop that attachment to the memory your cells will be more and more free. However, I do realize that on this 3D planet you are on a different level. If you are not there yet, I am not going to tell you not to take medicine. Sometimes medicine can help you, however you do not necessarily need this medicine, and sometimes the medicine can be harmful and it can hurt. It can prolong the process and cloud your cells. So the best way to not prolong the process is to sit with yourself and look at what the disease is and realize that if you just sit with the present moment you can drop a lot of that cellular memory from the past and not carry it with you into the future and into the present moment. You need to focus on the present moment and allow your cells to glow because that is what they want to do. They want to drop that memory. They do not want to attach themselves to a disease or to a memory. It is very simple to cloud your cells, like watching something on the television and then feeling like this is something that is going to happen to you. It is exactly like listening to music and you attach to something, which is why on my planet we are not too crazy about listening to music. You do not want your cells to attach to anything. They want to be free. I have come to this portal before and we do listen to some music, but it is very light and airy and something that we enjoy to do, but it is not something that we are attached to or say "oh we must come here, because when we come here that is what happens". You have to drop all memories and all attachments and it is the attachment to a particular memory that brings on a lot of these stressful and hurtful moments in your lives. You need to let them go. When I saw Betty I knew that she was struggling with some stuff and I also saw that she was dropping a lot of her cellular memory quickly because she had a glow to her and I could see that her cells were becoming transparent. Maybe that is a better way to explain it because cells are light and they will glow and they will become transparent. You can see through them. They are very translucent and it is a nice change that happens because your body becomes clearer and clearer and your organs become cleaner and cleaner. When your cells become clear everything that travels through your body is so much different. It is like the outside becomes the inside and the inside becomes the outside. Not sure if I'm explaining that correctly but if you spend your time in the present moment and have no attachment to any kind of disease or cellular memory your life will definitely change for the better. You will notice that you will not be as sick as you were before.

The other thing that you also need to pay attention to is that sometimes when your body is ready to make this change and jump to a higher vibration it pushes you even harder and harder. When you get pushed some things need to come to the surface and they come quickly. You may feel like you are getting all of these different types of ailments and when you get all of these different types of ailments they happen so fast and you are just clearing them. That is exactly what you need to do. Do not attach to any of these ailments. The quicker they come and the quicker you clear them, the ailments will not be as powerful as they used to be and not as tragic as they used to be. You are not attached to what the diseases might mean to you on a personal level as they used to be. That is something you are looking forward to. You want to remember that illnesses are memories that can go away.

I know that when we talked before, we have discussed a lot of the issues that you (Betty) are having now. I feel that you are clearing a lot of the diseases for the world. That is your job, and that is not an easy task that you are doing, but I think that you are handling it very well because as you come up with something new, the cells are not attaching to the idea of disease and the cells are just allowing it to pass thorough and you are clearing these illnesses for everyone else. It just flows through and it is supposed to and there is no attachment to it. So the best thing to do is the more you are being attached to the present moment, then you are on your way and you do not need to be connecting to illnesses or ideas in your head from your past or your future. You are just connected to the present and you are reacting to what is brought in the foreground for you. You just react to what is brought to your attention. There is no reason for you to attach to anything or start thinking that this is what that means or that is what that means because then you attach to a lot of fear. This is not something I even want to go into because I don't want to bring a lot of fear into this book. I want to bring a lot of light. I want to bring a lot of present moment information. I want to make it light and want you to realize that there is nothing to be afraid of. I don't want to discuss fear too much because I do not want you to attach to any kind of fear. What I want you to attach yourself to is the present moment, reacting to the present moment. I think you should attach your self to being able to relax in the present moment and then being able to go into nature and exchange with nature and the natural beings and the trees, the grass and not necessarily feel like if I do this then I can get hurt or if I do this I can get sick. That is not what nature intends to do. What nature intends to do is if you do attach to something it is there to clear you. You are having an exchange. You are helping each other clear and helping each other move forward by not attaching yourself to a meaning of any sort.

Nela: If one of our human cells contains the space to fill the information of 1000 books at 600 pages each, what is that space for once it is freed?

Red: That is a perfect example of attachment. Right there, it shows you how much information your body can store within one small cell. By allowing that cell to open up and expand and become light, that is pure consciousness. That pure consciousness is what raises your vibration and that is where you want to be. That is where the thinking will go away. That is where the diseases will go away because you have nothing that you are attaching yourself to. You want to be there, that pure consciousness. So if you can imagine how much space you have in your entire body for that consciousness to appear, for that consciousness to be and how long it takes for one particular body to grow that consciousness, it is an amazing amount of time. That is an amazing amount of space. So when I say do not attach to any kind of cellular memory that is why I say it. You want to allow that space to come through each cell. That is where consciousness is. That is where consciousness lives. So allow it to be. That is what light is, it is pure consciousness. You are not attaching yourself to a disease at that point or any kind of an emotion. You are not attaching yourself to anything. You just are. That is pure being. When you are in that pure being, you are experiencing pure joy. You are just moving in the flow. You are going from one place to another. You are not driven by anything but the flow. You are exactly where you need to be. You are pure life. You are existence and that is wonderful because you are in the oneness. You are in that flow. You are going. That is a good place. Right there in that example that you just asked me, that shows you how much space there is that is in one particular body.

Charlie: If someone looses a limb can they grow it back?

Red: No it is not possible for you to grow back your limb on this 3D level. There are other planets that you can do that but you are nowhere near there. What your planet really needs to focus on is letting go of fear and letting go of attachment to the meaning of something. So that is what humanity needs to focus on. I know that there is a lot of the reconnecting of limbs and there is nothing wrong with that because it is an exchange. You are exchanging with another human being and if that is what happens then that is needed to happen. There is something that might have happened in the past that needs to be reconnected. If nothing happens then that is the way it is. There is a reason for what ever is happening, so allow that reason to happen. So I would say if somebody has lost a limb and they need to have it reattached I would not say do not have it reattached. If the opportunity comes there is a reason for that to be happening. There is an exchange that needs to happen there, for what ever reasons we may not know. Maybe the cells needed to reconnect for some reason to be able to be full of space, to be able to become translucent and become light. This exchange is something we may not understand. Remember some of the things that happen in the world you do not understand and you do not need to understand. It is just that they are and it is it is just something that happens. It is not for the mind to understand, but it is something that your essence will understand and your essence will know exactly what it needs to do and how it needs to proceed.

Nela: Why is it that my head feels like it is being pressed and expanded and feels funky and it has for a few hours?

Red: My main reason and I hate to even tell you this. I think you are going to attach to it even though you should not. It is probably what's happening but try to not think about it too much. It is because you are carrying a higher vibration inside you and you are also talking to me a little bit more and you have not been around for a while. So, now that you have come and you have talked to me for a little while yesterday and today you are feeling the effects of my vibration. So it is something that your head is going to get used to. What is happening in your head is that you are probably loosing a lot of that cellular attachment to the past or the future and you are focusing on being more and more in the present moment. So when your cells are disappearing and they are turning into light they are becoming translucent. This loss of cellular memory can feel like you are in some kind of a pressure, a pressure that is squeezing you really tight, almost like a bursting of a cell. That is probably what you are experiencing. It is a bursting and just one burst of a cell can feel pretty messed up to you. So if you are having more then one burst in an hour or a couple of days that is a major feeling that you are going to experience. Now having me explain this to you, do not attach to it and say "oh that is what is happening to me". Just allow it to be. It is not something you want to attach to because it will get easier. As you come to me more and we discuss this you are expanding more and more and raising your vibration more and more and losing those cellular memories and turning them into light. You will notice that you will not be experiencing these symptoms any more. It will be just something that is and it will not bother you anymore, because there will not be any explanation or any reason for you to feel that way. It is just something that is known. Then your symptoms just evaporates into the isness of the world and into the universe and it is not something that bothers you any more or something that you are attaching to, not something that is needed to have an explanation and you move forward. That is probably what is happening right now.

Judgment

Charlie: We were talking about judgments. Judging is just something you do in the present moment and in my opinion judging is not bad. A lot of spiritual books say that judging is bad. I think what probably is bad is the blame that goes along with the judgment and the guilt. It is the holding of the blame and the guilt that is bad, not so much the judgment itself. Is this correct?

Red: I think that judging is something that you need to look at from a completely different perspective. Judging is something that you might be reacting to in the present moment. It is experience. As long as you are reacting to a present moment's experience then you are not judging. You are just reacting which is your natural reaction which is what you are supposed to do. For instance, if you have a plan to do something and you are saying "I want to get back at someone for doing something" then that is a judgment. That is something that you are doing that is very negative and that is something that you need to drop. Anything that is not happening in the present moment and you are using a lot of your mind to be thinking to do something, it could be considered a judgment. Anything is a judgment, "oh this is a beautiful day", that is a judgment, but if you are experiencing it in the present moment you are not really judging you are reacting to an experience. We talked about this before, where we have discussed if you hurt someone. Trying to save someone is reacting to an experience. Although as you get higher and higher in the vibration spectrum you are not going to want to have that reaction, but on your 3D planet do not look at it as a judgment, look at it as a reaction to an experience. Of coarse now, your ability to let go of that experience can be hard. Most of you will carry guilt, you are going to carry fear with it and this is just what we were talking about a few minutes ago. When you carry guilt and blame around, you are making yourself sick. You are making your planet very polluted with thinking. This is something you need to let go of. So as long as you are reacting to an experience, you are reacting in the present moment. But once you start thinking about something, then it becomes a completely different spectrum.

Emotions as Energy

Red: Today I thought about talking about emotions as energy. I think that on your planet many of the humans get energy confused with emotion. But when an actual energy comes through it is important to recognize what it is. Emotions are not something that can actually describe you or that can actually carry you into doing something that maybe you should or should not be doing. Emotions are not the driving force of right or wrong but many humans think this is so. So I think that it is very important to recognize energy as it comes through. Many times when energy comes through it can be in many different forms. Different energies can be mixed together, different types of energies that can stir up your emotions. You can think "oh wow this is what I'm feeling right now, a particular type of an emotion", but it isn't. It is all energy and it comes through.

Many times these huge beings called wave beings come through. They are these huge beings that basically come through the entire universe and they affect the entire universe. But they carry a particular energy with them and sometimes it is something that you may need to release and let go of. So there may be an interesting lesson that can come from these beings. So when these energies come through, recognize what the energy is, it could be the energy of anger or the energy of fear or any kind of energy and just let it go. Do not attach to it. Do not necessarily feel like in your thoughts that you need to make it into a reality. It is not. It is just an energy that you need to disassociate your self from. Realize what it is and not take it on as your own.

One of the most important things that humans need to learn is to not take things as their own. You sometimes will be in a crowd of people and there is a consciousness within that crowd. There is an energy within a particular crowd and if you are not careful to recognize what that energy is within that crowd you can start taking on that energy and feeling it and start reacting to that energy and thinking that this is something that is yours and not recognize that it is the energy of the consciousness of that particular grouping of people or that room that you are in, or a collective which is what you have on your planet and what we all have within the universe. So recognize what it is. Do not necessarily attach to any kind of energy just know that it is an energy, it comes through, and it gets easier. As you realize that you do not necessarily have to be attaching yourself to energy you will know how this energy will pass through you, it will pass around you and not affect you. And this is very important. It will get easier through time as you recognize what energy is and you will not feel this attachment to it and you will get better at recognizing it and that is all you need to know about that. It is just energy and energy just is energy and it comes from a lot of mental pollution, it comes from your thinking.

So you have the wave beings that will come and they need to bring something out of you, but at the same time do not forget that you also carry a lot of that energy with you, within your mind and within that mind you can create the feeling of a particular room or the feeling on this planet and you are somewhat responsible for that. So be careful what you are thinking. You do not want to expel a lot of fear and a lot of confusion. You want to have some clarity and you want people to realize that thinking is just that, thinking and there needs to be no attachment to it. So it is just energy. Be careful what it is that you are thinking of. You do not want to have messed up thoughts in your head. Just try to figure out how to live in that present moment. The present moment is your best answer because if you are in the present moment you are not confused with any kind of energy of the past, you are not confusing yourself with energy of the future. You are concentrating yourself on this present energy and that present energy just is the isness. You are resting in the oneness when you are in the present energy and that is one of the best things that you can do. Recognize that if you engage in thinking of what you think this might be then you can create a particular feeling and run off with it and that is not something that you need to be focusing on.

Charlie: Thank you that was very helpful. We had just left a friend's house and she gave us a hug and she has strange energy sometimes and my upper back and head felt a little funny.

Red: Do you think that was from your friend?

23

Charlie: I think that it may have been from my beliefs.

Red: So right there you saw that your thinking was something that might have gotten in the way and how this affected the back of your head?

Charlie: Right. It is like the combination of the two, the beliefs and strange energy from my friend, maybe.

Red: That is very good. Because it is that recognition of what it could be that is going to prevent you from attaching to something like that in the future. That is not to say that people do not necessarily have weird energies. People do have weird energies. It is just recognizing that it is not your particular energy and you do not need to mix with that energy. Recognizing that the energy does not belong to you and it is not part of your thinking, but it could be a part of someone else's thinking. Recognizing this is very important because it will get easier as you recognize that this is someone else's energy and that could be the energy of that particular collective, the energy of wherever your friend is from and whatever her collective is with her people and her general circle. They could be carrying that particular energy and that energy is something that could be affecting her immensely and you recognizing what it is and not attaching to it is very good. Although it did give you a pain it is nice to see that you just solved your own issue and said that this is what I believe that this is.

Nela: I kind of felt the last time I was here I was totally fried and now I feel incredibly wonky by being here, and you had said something about getting used to your energy and it will get better or whatever. But isn't that the same thing as what you just explained in recognizing what an energy is and not necessarily attaching to it?

Red: You are getting adjusted to my vibration. You are not getting adjusted to my energy. Energy can be caused by something that is thought and energy just is. It is the energy of life and the energy of beings. It is the energy of just existence. A vibration is something completely different. A vibration is on a higher level than what you are on so you are getting adjusted to my vibration. You are not necessarily getting adjusted to my energy. I do have an energy which is life and so does this planet. Everything around you has energy, because it is a living thing. Everything is alive so everything has an energy to it. A vibration is not necessarily that, vibration is not the energy. It is a level that everything has heightened to. It is like an energy that is not mixed together. A vibration is an energy that is settled energy all in one, all together. It is not different kinds of energy. Vibration is just one kind and it is pure and clean on a specific level. That is what vibration is and you are getting adjusted to the cleanliness and the clarity of the 15D which is really higher for you. You are getting used to handling it.

Stillness and Letting Go

Red: I want to speak about letting go and stillness and how difficult it is for humans on your planet to let go. They hold on to everything. You are holding on to your thinking. You hold on to diseases. You hold on to your loved ones. You hold on to everything and you can not ascend. You can not move forward. You can not grow until you start to let go.

The only way that you can let go is to reach a point of stillness. When you reach that point of stillness you become aware of what is going on and you become aware of what it is that you need to let go of. You tend to be attached to everything, like I have just mentioned. You are attached to a disease, if I have this disease I am what that disease makes me. You attach to your loved ones and they make you who you are when in fact that is not the case. No body makes you who you are other than yourself. What you need to do is go inward and figure yourself out, see what it is that comes up, recognize it and let go of it. This is not a process that happens overnight. It is something that you work on and you work on for a long time. It is not an easy process. It is not an easy process on any dimension. Everyone has things that they work on and they do. For you it is the emotional attachment to everything that you need to work on. Once you reach that point of stillness and you are quiet and you are with your self, you can notice what arises. All the things that arise that are negative or positive are all fine. It is in that recognition that you can see where your mind is going, where your mind is creating a thought of how something should be or to have a preference of an outcome and that tends to be a problem. When you have a preference and you want things to be a certain way then that causes a lot of pain on your planet. We do not have pain on my planet because we have let go of all of our emotional attachments.

Your number one emotional attachment is with your family, your kids, your friends, your loved ones, your spouse. This is only natural, but you attach to people before you are ready to attach to people. There is no maturity in your attachments. You do not attach to people like Krill and I do. We came together as one but we came together as one because we reincarnate together as one and we find each other and we are here to help each other move forward from one dimension to another. We raise our vibration together and up until the point until you find that particular one that helps you to raise your vibration, human beings attach to many other people thinking that they are the one that they are supposed to be with. In fact they are not the puzzle piece for them and therefore that causes a lot of pain and suffering. Not only do you bring on a lot of other folk's pain and suffering that does not belong to you but you also take on a lot of their mind garbage. So, when you recognize your attachments when you are in stillness, you can see them and you let go of them. You also do this with mothers and children and everyone that you surround yourself with. You recognize that everyone is on their own path and you let go of them. You recognize without trying to improve them or trying to tell them what they need to do because when you do you have a favor for an outcome and when you let go of that favor for an outcome then you are in stillness and then you can see how you are trying to change and manipulate your loved ones. What is going on with your loved ones is something necessary for their growth, for their development, for their movement into a different vibration and it is not your place to interfere.

At this point most of the humanity is where they need to be. Everyone is growing at their own pace and that is just fine. The one thing I always like to say is if you want someone to be a certain way you show them how to act and that is how people will be toward you. You be the role model. Be in that stillness. Be in that quiet time because that is where all of your awareness will be. You will realize what you are thinking and if what you are thinking is negative you are sending negativity for all to deal with. This is something you don't need to do. So by working on yourself and by letting go of all those things that you do not need anymore, you reach that point of stillness and you are that stillness and you are that awareness and you see where this is going to take you. You do not become numb. It is not that I do not have feelings for my girlfriend, my wife now. We have a different type of attachment, a mature attachment unlike human attachment. You do not have this attachment that you once used to have but it is a different type of an attachment. It is more clear and more pure. It is one of the most wonderful things that I have experienced and as you move higher on the vibration together this will also intensify for you. So the intensity levels change on things but you need to realize that by letting go of your thinking that gets in the way you will reach a higher vibration.

Ascension

I also wanted to talk about the word ascension and what that means. It seems that there is a misconception of what the word means. People think that it means that you are going to leave this human body and you enter something completely different. Ascension is not something that happens over night. It is not something that you just wake up one day and you say "wow I have ascended". This is not how ascension is. To me ascension means peace. To me ascension is working toward that inner peace and you recognizing yourself for who you truly are, the peace that is within you. So, when I say the word ascend, what I really want to talk about is how that word is misused and I think what ascend really means is peace. When you are peaceful that is the most important thing and as you grow and as you grow within yourself and you recognize all the issues that you have and you let go of them and you are in that stillness you achieve peace. This inner peace is the most important thing. It is not something that happens overnight. For some people maybe, but I do not think I have ever met anyone that has ever achieved peace over night. It is something that you work on. It is something that you strive for. It is not something that you have to struggle to achieve. It should come fairly easy, but the only problem is that we start to think and with all of that thinking that you have, that is what interrupts the peace that you are in. So if you can recognize that this way of thinking disrupts your peace and not get caught up in the word ascension and that you have to ascend, that it happens overnight and it is something that is going to feel great, then you are on the right path. Do not be trapped in this way of thinking. Realize that as this process is happening, you are achieving peace everyday more and more. You are being still with yourself more and more. You are recognizing when things arise and need to fall away more and more and this is exactly where you need to be. You need to allow things to grow, to show you the peace that you are and you will see it. You will see it all the time slowly. You will see it happen on a daily basis and you will see it happen more and more.

The way you show peace to people is by being that peace but not necessarily going out and starting a fight or reacting to an argument or doing anything like that. Just be the peace that you need to be and that shows them that they can not be anything else but peaceful towards you.

So the word ascension is what I just wanted to touch upon, that it is not something that happens so quickly and overnight and you are going to turn into light and glow. But it is something that happens gradually and the word that I would like to use is peace instead of ascension because it is a peace that you achieve slowly.

Oneness

Today I'd like to talk about oneness. It seems that there is a misconception on this planet of what that means. Krill and I were discussing this. How on your planet it seems that you guys have this theory that you are all the same, you are all equal. This is correct to a point but you need to understand what that means. The oneness is a huge universe and it all just is and it is an isness. It is something that is just happening all the time at once. What it really means is that one thing you do will affect someone else. On your planet you have this idea where you will say "oh we are all brothers and sisters" and yes you are but you will not see it the right way. You do not understand that what you do will affect your brother. What you do will affect your sister. What you do will affect your nature, the trees, the buildings, the universe, your planet, everything around you, the animals and insects. Even those insects, whatever they do will affect one another. The oneness is not about saying "oh we are all the same and what I see in me I see in someone else" but an understanding that what you do will affect someone else.

There is this interconnectedness within everything because your planet and the people on it affect everyone else. So for instance, if you have a war and I had just talked about nuclear weapons*, if humanity tries to explode weapons in the universe it is not going to work because that will affect everyone else in the universe. So we are not going to allow that to happen. But for instance you can do it to one another and that will affect one another on your planet. You will affect each other in doing that. It is greed. If you are greedy towards someone, they are going to be greedy back and that is also a oneness, an interconnectedness. It is the affect. If you are not going to take care of your planet it is not going to do well. It is not going to thrive. So it has to shake you off for the planet to be able to carry on and continue.

So this is what I wanted to touch upon. Just making sure that there is an understanding of what the oneness really means. That it is not when we talk about oneness that we are all the same, that we are all this happy group of people. What it is, is that what you do affects someone else. What happens in nature will affect you personally. So there is a connection between you, between nature, between everyone that you touch, everything that you do. That is why it is important to be loving and to be kind and to respect your nature and respect one another because that is where the oneness comes in. It is not about saying "oh wow this is my brother" and you not giving into the oneness and having this misconception of what it means but having a concept and the right meaning for what that oneness is. I think that there is a lot of people that say "oh they are the same as me, I'm not going to be mean to this person" and they should not be, but at the same time you need to remember that what you do affects someone else. The oneness does not mean oh we're all the same. At some point you are, but there are different parts of the oneness and these different parts affect one another. So your part will affect someone else and that is something that you need to remember, because the oneness is the big whole. It is the entirety. It is the isness. It is not saying that you on an individual basis are the oneness. You are a part of the oneness but the oneness just is. It just exists. You affect the oneness by what you do and how you act. So try to be loving and compassionate and try to be nice to your brothers and sisters and all the insects and all the beings on your planet. This is the most important thing to do. Your actions affect everyone else and they will affect your planet and your planet whether it is able to raise its vibration or not will affect everyone else in the universe.

We previously asked off the record if extraterrestrials would protect and stop humans from having a nuclear war. The answer was no. We humans can destroy ourselves but we are not allowed to use weapons in space. That is the reason why NASA's bombing of the moon to test for water did not work.

Charlie: What about when you step on an aunt and you kill one by accident? You want to be kind, but it is unavoidable to do certain things.

Red: This is something that just happens. It is something that happens on every single planet. It is not like you did it out of spite and you did it out of viciousness. You kill many insects that you do not even see and you are not even aware they were killed. There are beings that end their life cycle because it rains on your planet and you have a mass extinction. So it is not something that happens on purpose and do not forget that maybe it is time for that being to move on and to move forward and you just did an exchange with it. Maybe you did that being a favor. As long as it is not done maliciously you can see that there is an exchange that happened. I would say be kind. Wish that being a loving transitions and move on. You move forward too because that exchange is important to both you and for that being.

Charlie: Do you have anything to say about the way we treat and eat animals?

My biggest thing with animals is try to be kind to the animals. The treatment of animals can be very brutal on your planet and that is where the orbs come in and they help those animals transition. However I am not here to say you do not need to eat meat or anything like that because it is an exchange and you are exchanging with that being in a loving way as long as you do it the right way and the right way is for you to actually take care of that being the entire time. Now at the same time would I go out of my way and eat meat. No I would not. We do not believe in killing other beings on my planet, we exchange in a different way. However, you are killing everything, even the plants and vegetables on your planet are alive. They are all living so there is an exchange. There is a death that comes from that. So do not forget just because you do not see plants, fruits and vegetables walking around that does not mean that they are not alive. They are still alive and they are still producing, just like your tomato plants would be producing and they would have another one and another one. So it is the same thing with the chickens that grow and they have another chicken. So these are all the same things. It is just harder on your planet because your awareness is not as high. You see animals as more important than a plant that you might be killing and eating, but it is all the same thing. On my planet it is a little bit different. We see it all as the same and yet we exchange more than we actually eat. It is not something that we do because we are hungry. Eating is something we do for social events. On our planet eating may be fun for us to do but it is not something we do nearly as much as you do.

Orbs

Nela: Would you like to talk more about the orbs?

Red: Yes we do know that there are very cruel ways of killing animals on your planet. What the orbs do, they are of the highest vibration and they can transform themselves into anything on the planet and they are all over the place in the entire universe. So what they do is they will actually take the form of the animals and take the pain away so they are not feeling all of that pain. That is where the orbs come in. That is their job. They do that lovingly and the animals are not feeling the terror that they normally would have if these orbs did not come in and try to save them. So that is a very nice gesture on the part of the orbs. It is something that is necessary on your planet to witness, to be able to move to a different transition and transition to a higher vibration. It is important for your planet because it does not seem like the human beings learn in another way. You have to be shown terror and some people have to rise up and say this is not the right way and you move on. When you get to a higher vibration such as mine, then that all becomes very minimal. It is not something that we even think about or want to do. It is just something that does not exist. It is not part of our daily life at all. We have moved away passed that a long long time ago. And you will too, it will just take time.

Betty: Have you tried any of our foods?

Red: No I have not, but I do see it on the universal television and I see what you call it and what you guys have and you do not have. Some of it looks really interesting and cool.

Charlie: What is this universal television that you speak of?

Red: It is like when I previously told you that we watch your sports and we can actually tap into your systems. It is basically that. We can tap into the system of every single planet that is out there and watch what other beings put out there. So it is what you call technology. It is kind of fun for us once in a while, but we do not do it too often, but we do know about you in that way. It is a nice way to get to know your planet and the beings on your planet.

We spoke about universal television to Red before this and he told us he likes to watch our sports. He views it as a comedy because he said competition is silly to him. The concept of competition does not exist on higher vibrating planets according to him.

Charlie: How do you tap into universal television, with your mind or a machine?

It is with my mind. We do not have technology like that, that is a machine. We do not do that. It is a mind thing that we do. Remember when I told you how I found out where Krill was and to find out where she was and who she was. She is the one I am supposed to unify with so I need to be able to find her. Well, it is the same way. I lay down in nature and allow my mind to take me where I want it to take me and that is how I find out information.

Soul Mates & Family Units

Red and Krill had previously told us about their relationship. They explain themselves as two beings that had merged and united into one consciousness. Both of their families merge after they have their merging ceremony. Red and Krill say they have reincarnated lifetime after lifetime and have found each other each time in order to make their relationship and consciousness more pure. They say this is how we all merge back into oneness and raise our vibration to a higher level. We find our puzzle piece and merge with them. Apparently we are not doing a good job of this here on earth.

Nela: Since you have unified you had mentioned that you can take on each others abilities and the merging helps you reach a higher vibration. Does that make you stronger as an individual?

Krill: What it does is it enables both of us to understand each other better and it also enables us to have the different powers that Red has or that I do. So it would be the same thing on your planetary level. For example on a three dimensional level some people are more intuitive than others. So for instance Betty and Charlie have different gifts. Betty has more of the ability to see and speak to us and Charlie can feel and sense our presence. So if you two merged the abilities would be stronger for Charlie to be able to see and speak to us and Betty to feel and sense our presence. So these are the things that enable you to perfect on as you merge together with your partner, with your unit. Now this is not something that you can do with anybody. Only with your specific person, your specific puzzle piece. We have talked about the pieces of a puzzle before where as when you go back to the oneness, when you are re-submerging into the oneness everything is a whole. Everything is interconnected which I believe you talked to Red about before, but when you go back to the oneness you are supposed to go back in a specific way. So by merging with a particular person then you merge with your family which is already a merge because that is how you became. Then you are re-submerged into that oneness and you are becoming part of the whole again. So again you become stronger and stronger as you do that. It is like the little bits and pieces of the one coming together and reconnecting to go back to the oneness. The oneness is huge. It is all interconnected. It is everything. It is. It is this big isness that we have, that you have. The oneness encompasses all and everything. So by these little bits and pieces of the singular oneness, they come back to the oneness. It is like watching for example little bubbles and then these little bubbles coming together and connecting themselves. That is exactly how that would be.

Betty: Does that mean that you have to deal with family members who are difficult to deal with?

Red: It is difficult on your 3D planet and you have to remember that there are certain tasks that you need to do and certain ways that you need to be to raise your vibration and to get out of the 3D level. Now for that to happen you need to deal with certain people. These are the people who you will be dealing with on a very long term basis. These are the people with whom you will be dealing with as you keep going into different vibrations on a higher level. So by dealing with difficult family members on this level and by dealing with them now, you are not going to have to worry about it in the future. So you are better off to get it over with now and you do not have to repeat and keep redoing these difficult relationships again and again.

What you want to do is to try to relax into the relationship. See it for what it is. Realize what the exchange is and realize that when it comes to certain family members, which is very intimate it can be tough but worth relaxing into the relationship. It is very intimate on my level too with me and Krill but we have just unified our families and completed an even bigger puzzle, which means we became even bigger and stronger. We are going back to the oneness and that is an even bigger and even stronger thing to do and we will keep doing this as we rise into different vibrations.

So on a 3D level you feel like you do not want to deal with these people because they are a certain way. By not dealing with them and not learning the lessons that they are presenting you with and learning how to be and showing them how to be then you are going to just have to repeat it. So is it worth it? You have to ask yourself that or you will just figure out how to work on that level and see how you need to be. Basically it just goes back to what we were talking about the other day of just knowing what it is. Know what this energy is that the difficult family member is expressing and do not necessarily engage with it and then just move on slowly. Remember you are dealing with it in some way.

Charlie: So are you saying that if you do not engage with a difficult person and just relax then that may actually change the other person and we will be together for many lifetimes and our relationship will be peaceful or once we stop engaging we will learn the lesson and move on from that person?

Krill: No, what I am saying is that this person will be in your life as you keep moving from one vibration to another and it will change. It will have a different feel to the relationship and the relationship will get easier and easier just like the difficulties of the relationships here on earth. Why is it difficult to be in a relationship here on earth? Well, look at what you guys tend to do. You have a person that you are supposed to become a unit with and yet you ignore that fact and you keep looking to someone else and you try different people and these are not the people that fit your unit. You are exchanging with them and you never find that unit and you never learn how to move on and you are still stuck in that same pattern of doing something over and over again. In many cases some people find that unit and they still do not trust it and they are still looking to other people and this is how they dismember their unit and they go and try to be with some other people and then that does not work either. So now they have ruined that ability to change. They ruined their ability to move on and this is very difficult for the people of earth because you tend to have a complete mistrust of how the process works and the process is very simple if you just rest in it and let it come to you.

Everyone has their own little puzzle piece and when you find that puzzle piece and you complete it things get easier, things start to get smoother and smoother, they do not get more difficult. They get smoother in the relationship which is how the relationships around you will become smoother and smoother as well. Basically being a role model. It is not going to happen if there is mistrust which is very common on planet earth because people are constantly mistrusting and they are always looking for something better.

I believe that you guys have a saying that the grass is always greener on the other side. The person that they are with is never good enough. The person that they are with is not pretty enough or is not this enough or that enough and they are always looking for someone else. They are looking for a new person and that is not the way to grow and move on. That is ok if you are on that particular level and this is where you want to stay and you do not want to move on to a different vibration and you still want to engage in the 3D levels. Then that is ok, but we are getting to a point of a very big crunch where your earth is changing very much so and very quickly that these are the things that human beings should be paying attention to. It is a serious matter. It is not something to joke around about anymore because a lot of the people are not going to get that there is a shift coming about and that they need to start looking at things differently. You should be looking at life differently for humanities sake to be able to move on. Otherwise these natural disasters will continue and there will be a major shift and then there will be no choice but to look at life differently.

So there is always a choice. There is always something you can do about making a smoother transition. Yet it seems that majority of the people here choose not to do anything about the shift and choose to look the other way and choose to be engaged in some other things and choose to look to other people to complete them when that is not the case. Red and I are already complete and we looked for each other and we knew who each other were. We were complete as human beings, as beings from another planet and we are complete as everything. We started at a level where you are starting. We started at the same place and we grew to our 15th dimension, to our vibration. So by starting at a low base we know what that is like. We do not have a good memory of it because it has not been with us for a long time and the things that you deal with we do not deal with anymore. It is not part of our being.

There is no such thing as wanting to be with somebody else or desire. We complete each other in a completely different way and that is how the family comes into play as well. The family completes you in a completely different way. There is no bickering, there is no saying one should do this or the other should do that and I see that play a lot within the structure of your family on this planet. It will continue until someone puts a stop to it and the best way to put a stop to it is to recognize where you are and to recognize who you are with and how that is going to help you grow and how that is going to help everyone get to a higher level because you are not only affecting you. You are affecting everyone around you as well. It is not an easy thing to do but it is something to work on and it is hard on your planet but this is where you are and this is what you are dealing with right now. For us it was not that hard but we are also vibrating at a completely different level. We have given up the desire for listening to music and attaching to certain cellular memories to which you guys still have. We enjoy being here at this portal but it is for a different reason and I love to dance so I am going to but I am not attached to doing so. At the same time you guys are caught up in a lot of your cellular memories and the meanings of things. The meanings of things that are the meanings of a past love, the meanings of a future love, the meanings of what you have, the meanings of what you do not have, the meanings of gestures and the meanings of everything. When you drop all of that, then it is a completely different thing that you are dealing with. You go in a completely different direction and you are whole as a person and you do not need anything. Like Red and I, we do not need anything but we know that we enjoy being with each other and this is a completeness and we feel that completeness. It feels nice to be in that energy of the two of us and feeling the feelings and feeling the energy of the power that I have now that I have come into being with Red and the two of us being together.

Betty: What happens to a couple who are raising their vibration and does not want a materialistic life style any longer and are ready to move on, but their extended family still lives a very materialistic life? Their family still likes to have things, do things, want things and have many belief systems. Will the couple raise their vibration and leave their family behind?

Krill: No there will not be a divide. That is your family. That is part of your unit. You will make sure that they will raise their vibration. Your family, it may seem that they are not in the right line, but your family probably is at this point. What ever you have done and what ever your vibration is, your level, you being around them will actually change them very quickly. So it may seem that they are not ready for the shift but they probably are because at this point they probably do not even have a choice. If you pay attention to your family, are they going through major changes?

Betty: Yes.

Krill: So if they are going through a major change they are all questioning things, they are all feeling discombobulated. Then they are going to go through the shift very quickly and start to see things differently. They may not be as high as you, but they are probably ready to start on a new vibration.

Betty: How does it work if someone dies? How does a unit stay together?

Krill: When someone dies it is not like the same time for those who are living. Remember, time does not exist. So to them it could be a few seconds that they might have waited for the rest of their family to move on to their vibration. So it is really not even a question.

Charlie: Are friends included in the unit?

Krill: Mothers, fathers and children are the unit. That is your family. Friends have their own units to complete. Friends have their own purpose, their own lines. The way you are connected to your people is through an actual birthing or a conception.

Charlie: When you reincarnate as a family do the members come back as different sexes and different relationships such as a mother being the daughter and the daughter being the mom?

Krill: Not necessarily. You may have the exact same relationship. You just move higher and it will be an easier relationship. You may be looking very different. You may be from different planets, but you will still be connected in that way, just like Red and I came from different Planets.

Betty: Can a gay couple be a unit?

Red: Absolutely. They can be a unit.

Nela: How does that work since they do not have children and you have previously stated that a unit is mothers, fathers and children?

Red: Puzzle pieces connect in different ways. The way that gays can be a unit is the way puzzle pieces connect towards the edges. So they can be a unit. It is not specific and it is not completely set in stone that it has to be mothers, fathers and children, but for the most part it is.

Religion and Materialism

Charlie: I was watching TV last night and I came across a TV evangelist. He was saying that we are now in the season of not having to want. "God's gift" right now is, to those who are ready for it, can have the gift of not wanting. This sounds like what you say about the shift that is happening that we will not need material things and come into our true selves. Unfortunately at the end of the broadcast the evangelist turned it into a money thing. He said by sowing the seed of money you will receive this gift from God.

Red: I think it is exactly what he is talking about, the shift. I believe what he is talking about is the gift of yourself, the gift of coming together with your true self and the gift of knowing who you are and giving up all of the unnecessary thinking, giving up your ego self and that is the gift. As far as the monetary thing, I can see people on your planet still trying to cash in on things that are going on. As far as what he is talking about, I would imagine that that is what he is talking about. Because what other gift can you be talking about other than the not wanting anymore?

Charlie: What I found when he was saying give money to sow the seed was that he may have been offering the masses a way of trusting in "God's gift" of not wanting by giving away what they feel is valuable. So was he doing them a service?

Red: That is something I am not sure of but it sounds like you can take it either way. It is up to the individual for how they will take it. For some people he will be doing a service by giving them a chance to give away things that they do not need because you do not need anything. Everything you need is inside yourself. Everything you need is in nature. You do not need to have the things that you guys have. There is no need for material things. So by giving things away like money and material, it helps you understand that you do not need them. That is a gift for someone. Other people may still be playing with this 3D reality and may not be ready to do so. They are not ready to give. So in their ego self and ego mind if they do give it they may be very resentful and look at it in a completely different way. It is up to the individual. If the individual is ready to give up all the material and give up all the unnecessary then they are ready to move on. This will be a very big spiritual transformation for them. If the individual is not ready then there may be some consequences for that individual because they are not ready to give up their material possessions. That is a lesson that they need to learn. So it is a very tough thing to answer because you do not know where the individual is that might be going through this that might be listening to this man. For you, I would say being at the level you are at, if you gave, it would not mean anything. Because you know what it means. You know that everything you need is inside yourself and is inside of you. That is where he is pointing to. Although, some people may somewhat know that, but are not ready for it. So everyone is at a different level. You can not force people to be ready for something before they are ready for something. They need to learn and they need to learn how to let go of all that is trivial, give up all that is unimportant and to be able to be very humble with themselves and with others. You can not teach that. You show that. That is very hard to do because people do not necessarily like to learn valuable things on your planet. They like to have. They like monetary things. They like their money and their things. I have not seen many people here on your planet, who actually like to give.

Charlie: Do you agree that the gift of not wanting is available now and some will take it and some will not. Will those who do not take the gift have a hard time as the shift continues?

Red: I do not think that that matters anymore because everyone will be exactly where they need to be. It goes back to what we were talking about the other day that everyone is already in line to where they need to be. They are already divided. People are already where they need to be. They have either gotten passed that point or they have not. It may seem to you like they have not, but maybe they were in the right alignment in the first place. The right line is the right line for where ever they are. So, whether they take the gift or do not take the gift, that does not matter anymore. It is way passed that point. Right now it is at a point of it just is.

Enjoying the Now

Red: The now, the present moment is extremely important. Most people on your planet just think about their past. They think about their future. This is where the cellular memory comes into attachment as well and how important it is to be in the present moment and experience that present moment. This is exactly what I am talking about. Being purely in the flow and being pure consciousness because you are in the now. You are going from one place to another. There is no past, there is no future. You are in the flow. You are going from one spot to another. That is so important. Most people do not like that feeling because it does not give them the feeling of control. Most people like to control their situation. They like to control their outcome. Most people want to know what is going to happen. They want to know the reasons why. There is always a reason why something must be happening or why it is going to happen. How they perceive something to be happening. How they wish and want their life to be. They want a reason to be there. Enjoying the present moment means that you actually have to be okay with your self right now, you have to be ok with whatever is happening in that present moment.

Most people are not okay with that. So they try to escape it by being in the past or being in the future. But, if they only realized how wonderful that present moment really is and that there is actually joy there, very much light and love and wonderful things there, then, they would remain in the present moment. In order to get to that point they have to let go of a lot of their issues that they have in order to remain in the now. Sometimes it can take time but it is not that bad of a thing. You take the time, you clear yourself and then you achieve peace. That is where you want to be, in a completely peaceful state. Not in the past. Not in the future. Although, for most people, they need to have that reason of why something is just like when we talked about diseases. Why is this happening? This must be happening to me for a reason. If you are having a bad day you think that this must be happening to me for a reason. It is like the emotions of anger or some kind of negativity. "Oh but I am being positive, why is this person being negative to me?" Well, perhaps when you look deep inside yourself there is a reason. The reason is that you are being negative and you are maybe trying to hide it or you are negative and it is driving someone else's energy. As long as you are aware and you say "Oh I feel that energy, I know what it is", that happens in the present moment and that is how you get past that energy. That does not happen in the past, that does not happen in the future or looking for reasons. That happens in the present moment, when you realize that in the present moment, then you know how to let go of it. You are achieving peace.

Helping Others and Being a Role Model

Nela: what is your advice with helping people with their traps?

Red: I think people are exactly where they need to be. If they are asking for help you can give them advice. Although, be aware that just because you do they may not take it. To me I think the best way is to show them how to be. Show them how to act by your actions and not telling them what to do, necessarily. For instance this book, we had agreed that we would put it together but we are not telling people what to do. It is a suggestion. Something that you say well, this might be helpful if you want to read it. They do not have to. The book may do okay and it may not. That is not why you are doing it. It is a suggestion. See what happens with it. As far as telling people what to do and trying to help them, just do not attach to it and remember that some of them may not take you for what you are saying. They may not understand, they may not be ready. Everyone is already in their line. They know where they are going to be, so I would not worry about it.

Importance of Trees

Red: I wanted briefly talk about your trees. How it is important that you take care of them. It seems that on your planet you guys are very eager to cut down the trees and build things out of them and that is okay. But then when you do, you do not take care of those things that you built out of the trees. Now trees have been around for a very very long time and they help you grow. They help with your vibration. I think that sometimes you forget how important these trees are. I am talking about trees that have been around here for a long time, trees that just look like they are part of decoration and really small ones (we think he means bushes). Every single tree is very important to your planet. You can exchange with all of them. When I talk about exchange, I mean actually transfer really good energies between you and the trees. Be out there with your trees, be in nature and exchange with the trees and listen to the trees. Sometimes they have really good messages. They are beings that are very powerful and very wise and they should be taken care of. Sometimes you forget to take care of the trees. It is very easy for you to cut them down. You make things out of them, you build these things and then you knock these structures down.

Sometimes you are very mean to your trees in the way that you cut them down. I think that that is something that should be really known on you planet, that trees are very important. They are very special beings on your planet. They are not dead. They are living beings and they should be taken care of. You have trees that have been around for so so long and those are the most powerful trees. They give out vibration. They give out really good positive vibration. They house a lot of beings and a lot of life. They house you guys and that is something that you tend to forget. I wanted to touch on that briefly because trees are very powerful and they are very good teachers and teaching tools.

Dark Night of the Soul

Red: I would like to talk about the dark period. Sometimes it is hard to change from one vibration to another. All beings in the universe go from one vibration to another and that is how you change dimensions. That is basically what that means going from one dimension to another. As you move from one dimension to another each vibration has things that you lose, things that you do not need to hold on to anymore. The toughest part is that on earth, when that shift from one vibration to another occurs, it is such a new thing and it is one of the first times that you start to lose your attachment to the personality. This can be a very tough time for people. Normally when something like this happens you find yourself losing a lot of your personality and what you believe to be you. As you go through this period, sometimes it is very painful emotionally and it can be a very dark time for people. This is when on your planet a lot of beings go through depression and they are very sad and they have no one to turn to. This is a period where you are really left alone to deal with yourself, your inner conflict. No one likes to deal with their inner conflict and confusion on your planet. When this happens you are very alone and that is how it should be. Because in order to get rid of a lot of this attachment you have to allow yourselves to be able to glow you need to let go. The best way to do this is to allow yourself to be alone. As this period comes about, sometimes it can be very hard. For some people it lasts for a really long time, for some people it does not last as long. Once they realize what this process is, they let go of it and not attach to it. Just realize what is happening and move on. However, for some people this is very difficult. They get caught in this period and they do not know ho to get out. So there are a lot of times when people are going through the dark period and they are alone when things are leaving them and they just feel so distraught. They do not know how to get out of it. They do not know what is happening to them that they end up staying in that period for a very long time. They do not know how to get out. This is when some beings actually commit suicide. Which is not the way to go because then you will just repeat everything all over again.

However if you realize what you are doing and you recognize what is happening to you, then you know that you are going through this process of raising your vibration. The dark period will only last as long as you allow it to last. It will be as long as it is necessary for you. The dark period does not have to be so long, it does not have to be so turbulent.

The dark period is turbulent for the self because it does not recognize it self at first. The self does not recognize what is happening, so it goes through this period of complete dread. Once you realize what it is, it is easier to let the dread go. Now, as this is happening most people are very alone and are very sad and a lot of your fears and a lot of your anger a lot of your resentment, all of your negative self things that need to come up come up. This is when you have to face yourself. It is like facing your life right in front of you and it is very dark. All the things that you have done that you do not like and all of the things that you do not like about yourself will be coming to you. This is the time to recognize what that is, forgive yourself and move on. This is not a time to hold on to anything. Realize what is happening and let it go. Forgive yourself, forgive others, stop carrying the energies around that represent anger, resentment and fear and let it go. The longer you stay there the longer you will be in fear and you need to let fear go. You do not need to be so fearful. When this happens on your planet many people tend to go indoors and lock themselves up and this is a very difficult thing for them.

I would suggest if you realize that you are going through a dark period, recognize it. Go into nature more. Try to be outdoors. You do not have to surround yourself with people so much because this is something that you should be doing on your own, but definitely go into nature and start exchanging because it will ease up the process. The process works for everyone the same way for everyone on every dimension as you raise your vibration. It is just more difficult on earth because it is one of the first times you are doing this. It can be very trying and very painful but if you know what is happening do not allow the pain to come through. Allow yourself to grow and you will be fine.

Charlie: Would it be good to sleep and rest during the dark period?

Red: I would suggest that this is a great time to rest. This is the time when you should go out in nature as much as you can, just bring a blanket and lay down wherever you are. Whether you are among the trees, in the grass or on the beach, where ever you need to be. Just be outdoors. Give yourself plenty of rest. Drink lots of water. This is something that is going to pass through because it just needs to. It is an interesting phenomenon that happens because it does sort of happen quite suddenly for some people. It is not something that is so gradual. If you look back you can see some of the steps that you have taken that lead you to this period. However once it does grab you, you are in it and you are in it very quickly. When you are in it you can decide how long you have to be there for. You do not have to be there for very long, but most of you do not know what is happening so you get caught up in it for a long period of time.

How to Meet Light Beings and Astral Projection

Red: This is a fun topic that I wanted to talk about because I think that as people are reading this book they are going to want to know where we are located and how they can communicate with us. The best way to communicate with us is not the way that this group does. Because this group comes to a specific location where you can see us and we come through a portal. However, not everyone can come to this location and the majority would not be able to see us even if they did. So I suggest for people to contact us in the astral. Most of the time what I suggest to people is to just relax. Do not try to contact us. Allow yourself to be and allow yourself to explore. Drinking something warm is one of the best things you can do and just relax. It usually happens where you will astral project and not even realized that you have done it. Most people will project and they do not know that they have. They will be standing someplace and by the time that they realize where they are, they will get startled and they will wake up and they will not realize that they have astral projected somewhere. Astral projecting is not all that difficult. It is quite easy. It takes some practice at first. The best thing for it is awareness. Make sure that you are relaxed, have an intention before you astral project of where you want to be and who you want to meet. But after that intention let it go. Just relax into it and let it happen.

I can not tell you the best time of day to do it. It is different for everyone. Time is not really relative, so do it when you feel like you are ready to do it. Do not have any connection to it. Just try to relax and go where ever you want to go. I would suggest to astral project where ever you would like. I would even suggest to try to astral project as much as you can because it is quite fun. You can explore many different planets. You can meet many different beings. We had talked before about having planets that are also 3 dimensional that are a little higher in the 3D spectrum than yours that are different from your planet. This is something that you might want to explore. It is just that, something fun for you to do.

I do not want this book to be very negative for anybody. I am hoping this is quite fun for everyone to read. That is why I wanted to include this section and say it does not have to be all grim by allowing yourself to glow because you are losing your cellular memory and attachment. This can be a very painful process, but within this painful process I also wanted to say that there are very fun things that you can do. Even on your planet. That will make the process a little bit easier for you.

Charlie: I do not Astral Project very well and that is okay with me. Before I really wanted to and I was aggravated that I could not. I feel it is not a big deal if you can not astral project. Do you have anything to say about that?

Red: I think that you are in the right place because once you give up that intention of this is what I want and this is how I want it to be then things start to open up and happen. So I would not be surprised if you are astral projecting and from what I remember, we did meet up on different planets when we previously discussed doing this. It worked. It worked very well, especially with Nela. I remember seeing Charlie, but he just was not aware. He was in that state that I just talked about previously where you would astral project but would have no awareness that you were there. Many human beings astral project already, they just do not have the awareness when they are there of what is actually happening. Most of the time by the time you even catch it, you trigger something inside you and you are back. You are already back in your bed before you are realizing what had just happened. But you are unaware of it and do not remember it. Most people astral project very quickly. As soon as they close their eyes and they lay down they will actually astral somewhere far away, but they will not have any awareness of doing it. It can happen for a few seconds. It can happen for several minutes. You may have no awareness that this is happening to you.

Charlie: The reason why I was saying that it is not important is to comfort people who are having trouble astral projecting. It is not that big of a deal, as you said before peace within is where it is at.

Red: Absolutely, peace is something that all of the beings in all of the dimensions strive to be. It is most difficult for yours but you will get there. Astral projecting is just a fun part of being in existence that you can play around with. I look at astral projecting as a perk to being on a 15D planet where I can go from one place to another.

Charlie: You are not astral projecting here you are physically here, right?

Red: Correct.

The Sun: Our Nutritional Source

Red: I wanted to talk about how important the sun is to the entire universe. Right now I am really cold because I am used to having many suns on my planet. We have five to be exact and on your planet you have one. The sun gives you all of your vitamins and minerals and everything that you need to survive. It is one of your major sources of exchange. So try to be out in the sun as much as you can. Do not be afraid of the sun. Some people are afraid of the sun and they believe that they can catch a disease from it. This is not the case. It is your mind and your thinking that creates that happening, that disease. However, as I have said before, if you believe that the sun will harm you, you are better off being careful.

The sun also gives you information. Many times you will be doing something in your daily work and you will start to feel uneasy or a headache coming on, something that you do not feel good about. At that point the sun is sending you information. It is either clearing something inside your body or giving you information that you may need. The reason this is important is because this exchange with the sun gives you an idea of what is happening. The headache is telling you that this is a time to relax and stop doing what you are doing and allow the sun to give you the information it needs to. Sometimes when you get a major headache and you are in the middle of doing something and you do not want to stop, the headache will last longer and it will take the sun longer to give you the information. The sun's exchange will not be as easy for you as it could have been if you would have actually stopped, relaxed and allowed the information to flow through you. For example: when you are driving a car for a longer period of time and feel like you can not drive anymore and you need to stop. Chances are the sun has a download for you and you need to stop driving and get out of the car and relax and exchange with the sun for as long as necessary.

Many people do not understand this exchange with the sun and they will try to avoid it, when that happens you repel the information coming to you. Repelling the information is just going to prolong the process of you receiving the information and the information will go to somebody else. The sun will look for this information to be received by someone else. Try not to repel the sun. Realize that when you are having a headache or something is bothering you that it is not something major. Sit down, relax and close your eyes. It is time for you to just allow the sun to give that information that it needs to give and you need to receive it. That information could be clearing your cellular memory on different levels. It could be clearing a disease or useless information. It could be anything so allow it to be. This is a very natural exchange.

As I said the sun provides you with all of your nutrients and you may find that you do not even have to eat any longer. As you go out in the sun and you exchange with the sun you will realize that you are less hungry. You may find that you are not desiring food as much as you did before because you are receiving everything you need from the sun.

Many people on your planet live in many different areas. Some areas are warmer and closer to the sun than others. The information will be more intense in these areas. Be aware of your geographic location. The closer you are to the sun you may be getting more information and raising your vibration quicker and quicker. Just realize what is happening, allow the sun to send you this information and let it to pass through. Do not repel it. You are not doing yourself or the planet a favor by repelling the sun.

Charlie: Are we repelling the sun when we get sun burned?

Red: Sunburn is a belief system. When you think you are going to get sunburned or are afraid of the sun, it is your thinking getting in the way. Try not to allow your thinking to get in the way and you will be okay being out in the sun. However, as I said before, being on a 3D planet if you are not ready to allow your thinking to pass through and not engage and attach to it, then be aware and take the normal precautions that you would on your planet to protect your skin from the sun. I am not saying that you are not on this planet and that you are not dealing with your planetary issues. What I am trying to say is try not to attach to any belief system that will attach to your cellular memory where sunburn can be a cause and effect of being out in the sun.

Charlie: Are you hungry more on our planet because there is less sunlight than on your planet?

Red: No I get most of my nutrients from my planet.

Nela: There are people on our planet who will keep their windows and curtains closed. If we get most of our information from the sun and this is a good way to raise our vibration then what happens when you are not exposed to the sun?

Red: I think that many people on your planet who do that have this inability to want to move on. They are stuck in their own vibration. They are not willing to see life in any other way. They are very much inside themselves. What they are doing is refusing to allow the sun's rays to come through to penetrate. They are not taking on any information. What they are doing is repelling information. They are throwing it out there. They are not willing to accept it. I am not sure why this big denial is happening in their lives or what made them this way. I can only assume that they had a traumatic experience in their childhood or past lives that they are not willing to let go of. These experiences may be buried deep inside and they are not willing to look at them. By doing that they are not allowing the sun to come through.

When you feel fresh air, when you feel sunlight you feel better. When you are in that pain you do not want to feel anything else but that pain. The pain validates you. People do not have clarity when they are doing this, keeping themselves completely shut in away from everybody. I think that the best thing for those people to do is to go outside. Although it seems on your planet that is very difficult, the more you try to get them to go outside the more they will stay indoors. For most of those people they are dealing with many painful memories that they are unwilling to let go of. By allowing nature to come through, it is allowing peace to come into their lives and they are not ready for peace. They are ready for combat. They want to be warring with everything and everyone around them. It is not just on a personal level with them, but they are including people outside themselves as well. They want to be in a constant conflict because their bodies do not know what else to do and their minds do not know what else to do. They want to be in constant conflict. They want to have a constant fight. There is really not much you can do for humans like this. There is not a good way for them to raise their vibration unless they open up the windows and they go commune with nature. I doubt that anything will happen. They will be stuck repeating the same level over and over again for a long time unless they have a moment of clarity and they allow things to change for them.

The Elements

Red: I would also like to talk about the elements. Like the sun, they are also giving you information. For instance there is a lot of water on your planet and there is a lot of water in your body. The elements can create a major clearing. You will notice that many times when your planet is going through an emotional devastation there will be rains around the planet. The rains are an emotional clearing. Maybe you are feeling sad because you are experiencing an emotional clearing due to the exchange or information given by the rain.

Pay attention to the elements on your planet. You also have the wind. It is very windy today. Make sure you sit and listen to the wind. The wind will sometimes carry messages and give you downloads and give you information. So you are getting information from all sorts of levels on your planet. You get information from the sun and all of the elements. You just have to sit and listen, you have to be still and realize what is going on.

Fire is another element to pay attention to. If you look into it, it will give you information. Many people have a lot of visions while exchanging with fire on your planet. They may be past life experiences, a clearing or future information. These are things that will cause you to relieve your cellular memory and be in the present moment and not attach to anything. Connect to the earth. All of these things around you are giving you information. Do not neglect them and do not think that they are here for no reason. Be aware of all their information because they are here to give it to you.

By repelling all of this information you are tossing it away to someone else and you are not raising your vibration. All of these major exchanges are super important because you are helping yourself clear cellular memory and any kind of attachment. It helps you be in the present moment especially and it is a good way to raise your vibration.

Cellular memory clearing is one of the key elements for your entire body to be able to glow and allow that space to happen for you to achieve living in the present moment. So try to be aware of what element is happening mainly in that particular moment and your particular time and see what it is that is clearing from your body. Be present, know what is happening. Know that when it rains there is a reason for the rain. When it is windy there is a reason for that too. Do not attach to it, but be aware of what is happening and do not be afraid to exchange. Many of these element changes will cause pain in your body somewhere because those are the particular areas that need to be cleared and to need to have the attachment of something let go. So allow that to happen and many times by you not allowing that to happen, it will cause it to be either more painful or you will attach to it more. So allow the exchange to happen. Allow the clearing to pass through and allow it to go. All of this is a part of the raising of your vibration and allowing your cellular memory to be cleared. Allowing a new space and allowing that space to glow.

Meditation

Red: I think it is important to bring up meditation. When I ask you to exchange with nature and fellow beings that means to allow the exchange to happen as you are meditating. A lot of the times you can not go outside and many of you have the excuse of being busy and can not spend time outdoors. A good way to raise your vibration is to meditate on your own and be quiet with yourself. Sometimes people do not like to do this because when you are quiet with yourself you have to face yourself. That is one of the biggest hurdles of meditation. Of course a good way to raise your meditation and vibration is by facing yourself.

When you face yourself a lot of things come up that you might not be ready to deal with. Sometimes when you meditate you get glimpses of other worlds as well. Meditation can be fun, but it takes some time and practice to get to that point. If you are just sitting quietly with yourself sometimes you will notice that you will see many colors, you will see tunnels. It is like traveling through portals and you are being shown different worlds. That is the fun part of meditation. Then there are parts of meditation when things come up that you may not be ready to face. When for instance you are remembering something that might have happened in your childhood that you may not be ready to face, you may have a very strong aversion and not want to go through with the meditation. However, if you stay quiet and you just listen and allow all of that childhood memory to come up and dissolve then you do not attach to it. I would recommend that everyone do this more than once a day because if you do this you will be raising your vibration in a much smoother way and dissolving your fears. The stuff that you are not willing to face will come up but as long as you do not attach to it and you realize what it is you will be okay. Sometimes things will come up from your past that you are not even aware of. I mean the past from other lifetimes and they may scare you and you may not even recognize them for what they are. That is okay. Know what it is and let it go. Sometimes you will be in a meditation and you will have a feeling that is very uncomfortable and you just want to get up and run away. That is when it is the best time to sit with it and feel that feeling and allow it to be and allow it to pass. That is the only way that you can let it go and let it move on.

This is how you achieve clarity. By allowing all of these different things to come up, you face them, you let them go and then you start to see clearer and clearer. You kind of develop a sense of knowing who everyone in your life is and what everyone's role in your life is. You do not have this misconception of what their job is in your life. I think that meditating can be fun at times. At first it might be a little tough because you are not ready to face yourself. However, if you do face yourself you will experience many benefits and clarity is one of the major benefits to facing yourself.

As you keep meditating you can achieve things that we have discussed before, like astral projection and you can check out different portals and travel through tunnels and see different colors and different worlds and beings. Those are all different fun things and perks to meditating. I would recommend that you meditate a couple of times a day until you get used to it and you clear yourself. If you focus on doing this and more people on your planet would do this you would have a very peaceful planet. You would achieve peace.

There is not much peace on your planet. Everyone is very angry and everyone is very nervous and resentful and they are not sure why. If everyone would just sit down and face their own self then they would know why. Some of the times when you are facing an angry feeling it may not even be your own angry feeling and that would be a good thing to recognize. You may be carrying an angry feeling from two lifetimes ago and not even realize that it is a feeling from two lifetimes ago. It is not something you should attach to. This angry feeling is something to let go of. But if you do not sit with your self and you do not have that clarity to realize where this feeling is coming from, you will not know how to heal yourself.

This is also true with disease, you might be feeling a pain from an injury from a lifetime ago and you do not realize it. You do not know. You think that this is a pain you have right now and you are not willing to deal with it. If you sit there and meditate and feel the feelings, it may come up as a very fast vision or you may have an ah hah moment or a realization of how that pain might have occurred. You do not attach to it and you let it go. That is how you move on.

So that is what I wanted to say for today. Just focus on getting some meditations into your daily routine. I do talk about exchanging with nature and I think that that is extremely important, but I think that meditation might be something a little bit closer and easier for people to do on your planet and then move on to exchanging with nature. I would recommend doing both, however if meditation is a little bit easier it may not be something that is so enjoyable at first, but it is something that I would highly recommend for everyone.

Past Life Injuries

Charlie: I have read somewhere that freckles and birthmarks are injuries from past lives. Is there any truth to this?

Red: No, that is not true. Freckles are not signs of injuries from a past life. Injuries from a past life come in a very different way. They will appear as energy. Most injuries will come as energy and it will lodge itself somewhere in your body. Sometimes this energy will go where it has no reason to be. It may be that you were in a war and you were injured on your leg, but for some reason the energy has come in and settled in your head. There is no reason to how the energy travels. The best way is to allow this energy to pass through. This is why I say exchange with nature. Just relax as much as you can and do not pay attention to that injury. Try not to put a label on the injury and say this is what it is, because if you remember that cells need light and they are letting go of any kind of attachment that is all energy. Nothing is solid. You are not solid.

Letting Go of Tools

Charlie: You spoke to us about tools before. Can you revisit the conversation? We spoke about things like yoga, spiritual and religious books, Reiki and energy healing and pretty much any other spiritual practice, objects including so called spiritual drugs like salvia.

Red: Everything that you use is a tool. It is something that you use for a short period of time and you allow it to pass away. Meditation also is a tool and stepping stone to get from meditating to nature and exchange. The best thing to do is to recognize that what you are using no matter what it is, is a tool and that tool will be with you for however long you need it. One day when you do not need a tool you will be able to raise your vibration on your own. So I would recommend that as long as it is a tool and it is helpful, use it. Remember that you are on a 3D planet and tools are what you use for the moment. When you are ready to move on you will not need to use tools any longer.

The Energy of Domination and War

Red: I would like to talk about how people like to dominate one another. Be aware of that energy that is here on your planet. It is a power play and it is one that needs to be lost. For example you have wars and it is all because you are trying to dominate one another. At the same time you are trying to dominate each other in relationships. In intimate relationships, extended relationships, even with your pets you do the same thing. If you have the awareness that there is nothing to gain from someone else and everything that you need is inside you, it is a good way to drop that dominance. However, it seems very hard for humanity to do. You are not aware that everything that you need is inside you and this dominance power play is all ego-based and it is some kind of an attachment to something. You do not feel good, so you are trying to feel good through someone else, or you do not like something and you are trying to take energy from someone else. It is never a genuine relationship. It is usually one person trying to get something from someone else, or trying to achieve something. There is always a doing behind it.

I think that it is important if you are aware that you are in that type of a situation that that is what is happening. When you have that awareness of that energy play it is easier for you to drop it and not attach to the situation. Simply remove yourself from that situation if necessary. Many people are stuck in relationships like that for a very very long time and they do not realize what is actually happening. That someone is either draining them or overpowering them. It is just an energy play, but they are not aware of it. If both parties were aware of this energy play it would be dropped. But so many people on your planet are using this energy play that it becomes such a part of your collective that it is very much inside of everyone. So I think that dropping a lot of that attachment and knowing where this is coming from is the key to not being so dominant.

Also, people on your planet seem to think that if you are dropping that dominance and not attaching yourself to an ego that that is some sort of a weakness. That is not the case. There is no weakness there. If anything you just realized that the power lies within you and that is all that you need to know. Inside of you is where you get all of your power. But people do not trust themselves enough to know that the trust you need is inside you. It is not in someone else. You do not necessarily have to trust someone else. You have to trust yourself.

So, when you find yourself in a situation where you are trying to get something out of someone or dominate someone, realize what it is and realize that there is nothing that that person has to give you. They have nothing to offer you. Everything you need is inside of you. Drop that relationship dominance because it will not get you anywhere. That type of a relationship will not complete you. It will never be enough. So keep in mind this dominance and how you are playing this energy out because it really is not worth the time. It will only keep you lower on the vibration level.

Self Empowerment and the Meaning of Things

Red: The other thing I wanted to touch upon is meaning and how many times you attach yourselves to the meaning of something. You assign meaning to everything. Not only does this cause disease as we mentioned previously, but on a level of "I can not do this because it means I am a bad person" or "I am going to do this because it means I am a good person". There is no meaning behind anything. If anything, look inside yourself, see what you feel the right answer is for you and go with that. When you are looking for some sort of a meaning you are looking for something outside of your self. Looking outside of your self is not the answer. Believing in yourself and trusting yourself, which is very hard on your planet, that is where everything lies. When you believe in yourself you can drop the ego, drop desires, drop the meaning behind something, drop what you want or drop what you are trying to get and achieve. Just let it all go. Do not attach to it and look for the trust within you.

Now that is something that is super hard on your planet because no one is looking for the trust inside themselves and no one knows how to trust themselves. There is always second guessing, there is mistrust, a lot of negativity and of coarse it comes from the thinking. If you allow all of that to come into play and allow it to be a part of you, you are going to be very negative and you are not going to move up on the vibration level at all. But, if you realize that a lot of what you are thinking turns into an emotion and then it turns into something that you are feeling in your body and all of a sudden you start to seek, you are then seeking outside of yourself. That is not where the answer is. The answer always lies within you. There is nothing to seek outside of you. Everything you need to seek is inside of you.

Have that awareness of where this is coming from. The energy play of dominance or the meaning of something or the seeking and wanting of completeness to come from outside of you, these negative energies come from thinking. Thinking is the issue. Once you start thinking and you go into this pattern it is hard for you to turn it off. At the same time, here you are thinking something completely negative and then you do not feel good, immediately what you want to do is, you want to find someone else who does not feel good or find someone else whom can make you feel good because you think that person has what you want. Nobody has what you want. What you want is inside of you. That is one of the hardest things for humanity to understand. That what you have is inside you and not to look outside of yourself. Everything that you need is within. Go within. Sometimes that is one of the hardest things to do.

Going within forces you to settle down with yourself, it forces you to look inside and get rid of a lot of the junk and the thinking and be peaceful with yourself. When you become peaceful with yourself everything else around you changes.

Many times we are not peaceful with ourselves. We are looking for everything outside of our selves and we forget the peace that we are. You forget the peace that you always are, that is always there and has never left you. Peace has always been there and you have always been that peace. Somehow all of the thinking and a lot of the desire, the wanting and looking outside has buried the peace. But if you just sit with yourself and are quiet and allow that thinking and energy to come through it will not stick to you and cause pain or disease and that is all you need to know.

This is how I would like to end the book. I just want people to know that looking outside is not the answer. Everything that they need is inside themselves and just be peaceful. It is a very simple message. Stop looking elsewhere because you are not going to find it anywhere but in yourself.

Charlie: Is that the same as saying trust the god within you or trust the awareness that you are instead of the personality and the thinking?

Red: It is all semantics. You can use the language that you choose and that better fits you. Many people understand words differently. So hopefully whatever is meaningful to them and I use the word "meaningful" because there is no other way for me to express this. What ever feels right to them God or Being or Peace or Love, then that is what they need to use. And that is okay. I think people should know that it is all the same and it comes down to semantics. People can use different words to understand things differently and at the same time it all means the same thing. We are exactly the same. We are all part of the oneness. It is just how you portray that oneness. It is hard to explain what the oneness is because you can say it so many different ways on your planet alone, so can you imagine how many ways you can say it in the universe, on different dimensions. It is different things to different people, but it is all the same. So it is however you understand it and however you can connect to it and just joining back into the oneness, falling back and joining the flow. Once you are in the flow then it is easy. It is all semantics from that point up to the flow.

Note: The text in this book has been stream lined for conservation of paper.

This book was produced by NELABOOKS.

Please visit our website to find more interesting books.

www.nelabooks.webs.com

Become our friend on facebook

www.facebook.com/nelabooks

© 2010 NelaBooks

12661000R00040

Made in the USA
Charleston, SC
19 May 2012